ANIMAL CANNIBALS

Black Widow Spiders

Sam Hesper

PowerKiDS press.

New York

Published in 2015 by The Rosen Publishing Group, Inc.
29 East 21st Street, New York, NY 10010

Copyright © 2015 by The Rosen Publishing Group, Inc.

First Edition

AUG 0 3 2015

Editor: Caitie McAneney
Book Design: Michael J. Flynn

Photo Credits: Cover Jay Ondreicka/Shutterstock.com; pp. 5, 7, 18, 22 (black widow spider) Peter Waters/Shutterstock.com; p. 7 (grasshopper) anat chant/Shutterstock.com; p. 8 IrinaK/Shutterstock.com; p. 9 Brberrys/Shutterstock.com; p. 10 Colton Stiffler/Shutterstock.com; p. 11 Matteo photos/Shutterstock.com; p. 13 © Snowleopard1/iStockphoto; p. 15 (orb web) Isuaneye/Shutterstock.com; p. 15 (black widow web) Scott Camazine/Photo Researchers/Getty Images; p. 16 Cathy Keifer/Shutterstock.com; p. 17 Crystal Kirk/Shutterstock.com; p. 19 Nate Allred/Shutterstock.com; p. 21 Natures Images/Photo Researchers/Getty Images.

Library of Congress Cataloging-in-Publication Data

Hesper, Sam, author.
 Black widow spiders / Sam Hesper.
    pages cm. — (Animal cannibals)
 Includes index.
 ISBN 978-1-4777-5748-2 (pbk.)
 ISBN 978-1-4777-5828-1 (6 pack)
 ISBN 978-1-4777-5745-1 (library binding)
 1. Black widow spider—Juvenile literature. I. Title.
 QL458.42.T54H47 2015
 595.4'4—dc23
                              2014024164

Manufactured in the United States of America

CPSIA Compliance Information: Batch #CW15PK: For Further Information contact Rosen Publishing, New York, New York at 1-800-237-9932

Contents

The Black Widow

Are you afraid of spiders? Many people are, but you shouldn't worry about them too much. Spiders are afraid of you, too. However, there's a good reason to be afraid of black widow spiders. When black widows catch **prey** in their webs, they **inject** the prey with strong **venom** to **paralyze** it. Then, black widows eat their prey. They're fearsome predators, and they even eat each other sometimes! That's called cannibalism.

Unless you're a bug, you're in luck. Those small critters are a black widow's favorite meal. Also, the biggest black widows are only 1.5 inches (4 cm) long, and you're a lot bigger than that!

Black widow females are mostly black with red markings on their body. Even if they don't want to eat you, it's best to stay away if you see one.

Arachnids

Black widows, like other spiders, aren't insects. All spiders are arachnids. Arachnids are related to insects, but are different in several ways. First, insects have three body **segments**, while arachnids have two. Insects have six legs, and arachnids have eight. Insects commonly have wings, and arachnids don't. Insects have feelers on their head called antennae, and arachnids don't. Ants and grasshoppers are examples of insects. Spiders, scorpions, and ticks are examples of arachnids.

Scientists observe the **similarities** among different animals and plants to explain them. Noting the differences between **organisms** helps scientists describe them, too.

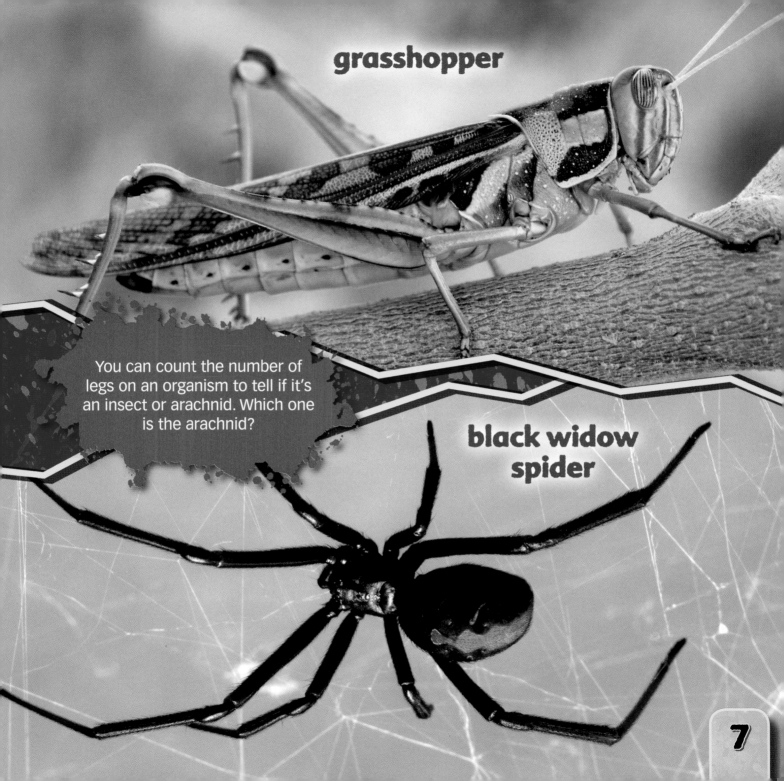

grasshopper

You can count the number of legs on an organism to tell if it's an insect or arachnid. Which one is the arachnid?

black widow spider

7

Spiders and Latrodectus

An important feature of spiders is that many spin sticky webs to make their home. Spiders have a pair of pinchers at the sides of their mouth called pedipalps, which help them grab prey. They use their sharp teeth, called fangs, to inject venom into the prey, paralyzing it.

Black widows are members of a group of spiders called *Latrodectus*. Scientists put more than 30 kinds of spiders in this group because they all inject their prey with strong venom. Black widows are the most famous *Latrodectus* spiders because their venom is very powerful.

FOOD FOR THOUGHT

Spiders have 48 knees! There are six joints on each of the eight legs.

Spiders spin webs out of silk. Black widow silk is the strongest of all spider silk. Many black widow spiders stay in their web and wait for the sticky thread to capture their prey.

9

Where Do Black Widows Live?

Three types of black widow spiders live in the United States, but they all look very much alike. Black widows live in most U.S. states. Many other black widows live worldwide, and they live on every **continent** except Antarctica. Some black widow cousins are the redback spider of Australia and katipo of New Zealand.

FOOD FOR THOUGHT

Black widow spiders are solitary, which means they like to be alone. They only come together to **mate.**

Black widows live in **temperate** areas of six continents because they like warm places. They like to live in quiet and dark places, such as under rocks and in holes in trees. They usually come inside only when it's cold. You might find them in crawl spaces and basements.

Mediterranean black widows are found in many European and Asian countries. They have 13 spots on their body that are usually red.

How to Spot a Black Widow

Female black widows are easy to recognize. They're black with red markings on their **abdomen** that are easy to spot when they hang upside down. Sometimes the markings are more orange or yellow. Black widows found in North America have a red marking in the shape of an hourglass. Scientists think black widows are so easy to spot because that keeps predators from attacking them. Birds or wasps may not attack a spider with such powerful venom.

Male black widows are smaller than females. Males are usually lighter in color, but they may still show the markings.

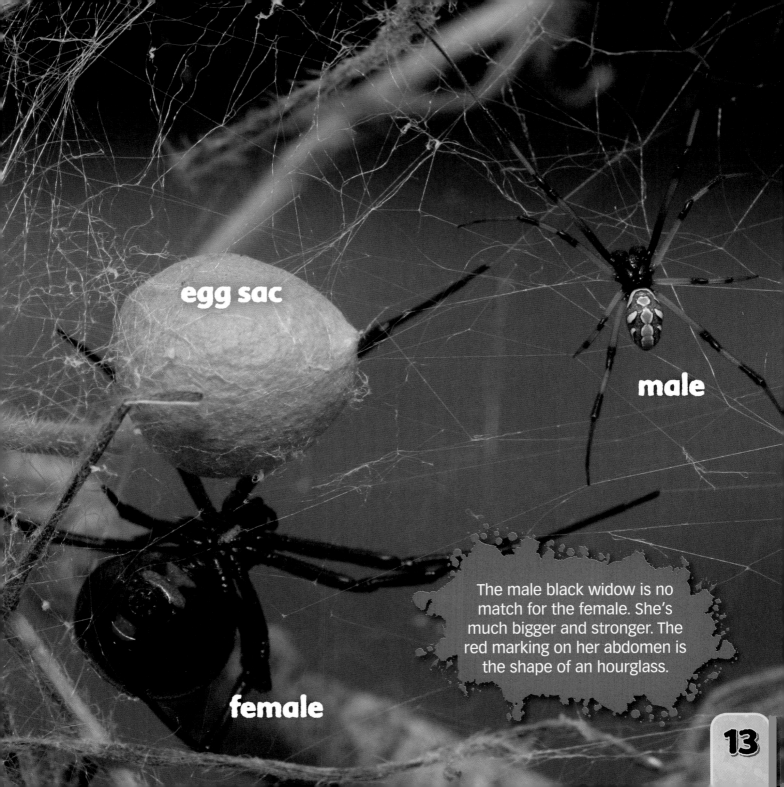

egg sac

male

female

The male black widow is no match for the female. She's much bigger and stronger. The red marking on her abdomen is the shape of an hourglass.

Black Widow Webs

When we think of a spiderweb, we normally think of an orb web. An orb web looks somewhat like a bicycle wheel.

Black widows make different webs. At first, a black widow's web looks like a messy collection of silk, but it has three important parts. The first part is made of supporting threads, which might be on top of a pile of rocks or wood. The second part is a tangled web that's good for hiding. The last part of a black widow's web is a sticky part to trap prey. The black widow hides and waits for an insect to get caught in the web.

FOOD FOR THOUGHT

Scientists believe black widow silk is five times stronger than steel!

black widow web

This spider made an orb web. It follows a certain pattern. A black widow's web seems more tangled. This kind of web is often called a cobweb.

The Black Widow Diet

Do insects taste good? Black widow spiders think so! They hang upside down on their web and wait for an unlucky insect to get stuck. Black widows will eat any insect that gets trapped in their web. They'll eat moths and flies as well as wasps and caterpillars.

But black widows, like other spiders, don't actually eat insects. They drink them! First, they wrap the prey in sticky silk so it can't move. Then, black widows inject a **chemical** into the prey. The chemical turns the prey's insides into liquid. Then, the black widow drinks the guts like a milkshake!

praying mantis

FOOD FOR THOUGHT

Some praying mantises and wasps are known to snack on black widows.

Spiders don't get caught in their own web because they can spin silk that is sticky and silk that isn't sticky. Spiders are sure to step only on the nonsticky silk. That takes a lot of skill with eight legs!

17

Powerful Venom

A black widow's venom is nearly 15 times as strong as a rattlesnake's venom. That's very strong! Luckily, a black widow makes venom only so it can paralyze and eat insects.

Black widow venom is deadly for insects. Black widow bites can also be deadly to small children, older people, or people who are sick.

Black widows don't want to bite people. However, they will bite people if they feel afraid. These bites are painful. They also cause dizziness, fever, and bad aches and pains. A bite is rarely deadly as long as the person gets medical attention. It's important to treat a black widow bite quickly. Doctors will give you medicine called antivenin that treats the pain and stops the venom.

Snacking on Spiders

When it's time to mate, male black widow spiders find a female black widow. First, the male taps on the female's web. It's his way of saying, "I'm not a fly caught in your web. I'm male, and I'm ready to mate. Please don't eat me."

If the female black widow likes the male, she'll let him onto her web to mate. If she's hungry after mating, she might eat him! Then, the female lays eggs and wraps them in a silky covering called an egg sac. A black widow egg sac holds hundreds of eggs. Baby black widows are called spiderlings.

FOOD FOR THOUGHT

A widow is a woman whose husband dies, which is where we get the name black widow. However, black widow cannibalism happens more often in labs than in the wild.

If the mother is hungry when the spiderlings are born, she may eat a few. When the spiderlings are hungry, they may eat their siblings. The cannibalism starts right away.

21

What Should You Do?

Black widow spiders can't catch you in their webs, paralyze you with venom, or turn your insides to liquid. They're still dangerous sometimes, but the good news is that they want to stay away from people. Why? We tend to wear big shoes and carry books and flyswatters that are good for squashing spiders.

If you see a shiny black spider with red markings on its stomach, stay away. That's what they want us to do. These creepy crawly cannibals don't have a taste for human flesh. But insects, males, and spiderlings are out of luck if the female is hungry!

Glossary

abdomen: The large, rear part of a spider's body.

chemical: Matter that can be mixed with other matter to cause changes.

continent: One of Earth's seven large areas of land.

inject: To force something into the body.

mate: To come together to make babies.

organism: A living being.

paralyze: To take away feeling or movement.

prey: An animal that is hunted by other animals for food.

segment: A part of something.

similarity: Something that things have in common.

temperate: Not too hot or too cold.

venom: Poisonous matter an animal makes in its body.

Index

A
antivenin, 19
arachnids, 6, 7

B
bites, 18, 19

C
cobweb, 15

E
eggs, 20
egg sac, 13, 20

F
fangs, 8
females, 5, 12, 13, 19, 20, 22

I
insects, 6, 7, 14, 16, 18

K
katipo, 10

L
Latrodectus, 8
legs, 6, 7, 8, 17

M
males, 12, 13, 19, 20, 22
Mediterranean black
	widows, 11

O
orb web, 14, 15

P
pedipalps, 8
predators, 4, 12
prey, 4, 8, 9, 14, 16

R
redback spider, 10
red markings, 5, 12, 13, 22

S
silk, 9, 14, 16, 17
spiderlings, 20, 21, 22

T
types, 10

V
venom, 4, 8, 12, 18, 19, 22

W
webs, 4, 8, 9, 14, 15, 16, 17,
	20, 22

Websites

Due to the changing nature of Internet links, PowerKids Press has developed an online list of websites related to the subject of this book. This site is updated regularly. Please use this link to access the list: www.powerkidslinks.com/ancan/bws